# Sonnets for an Analyst

## Other books by Gladys Schmitt

Gladys Schmitt

# SONNETS FOR AN ANALYST

with an introduction by Peggy Knapp

Carnegie Mellon University Press
Pittsburgh 2004

Library of Congress Control Number: 2003112555
ISBN 0-88748-421-2
Printed and bound in the United States of America
First Carnegie Mellon University Press Edition, 2004

10  9  8  7  6  5  4  3  2  1

*Sonnets for an Analyst* was first published by Harcourt
Brace Jovanovich in 1973.

The publisher would like to thank Dan Josephs for his
assistance in the publication of this book.

# Introduction

I find these poems beautiful, and I have ever since I read them soon after their publication in 1973. Gladys Schmitt was quoted as being reluctant to release them, not because of their autobiographical content, but because they were couched in a poetic form the 1970s seemed to find unfashionable. We look at these poems now in a different critical context; some of the most eloquent writers on art and literature today defend the control of form as that which distinguishes art from other forms of discourse. Denis Donoghue, for example, argues that the form of a successful poem causes an immediate, felt reaction, but in addition invites the sort of reflection that carries us beyond the situations and persons it describes. In a seeming contradiction, its power to reach beyond its personal and historical boundaries is precisely its formal "boundedness." The sonnet is surely among the most narrowly bounded of poetic forms, and Schmitt's use of it adheres to yet other elements (dialogue and allusiveness) of its traditional form.

Although all of Schmitt's nine novels contain autobiographical elements, *Sonnets for an Analyst* presents the fullest picture of her rich and passionate responses to the world of experience and the world of language. Like T. S. Eliot's, Schmitt's work regards poetry as an escape from emotion rather than an indulgence in it—or rather as a victory of form over confusion. Poetry may or may not produce a literal record of events, but it does create an image of their meanings in a virtual way. The virtual world of these sonnets, though, does seem to have been fashioned during the course of her psychoanalysis, and therefore reflects on the psychoanalytic process and the "convoluted chambers" of her own brain. Lois Lamdin ("Out of Despair" in *I Could Be Mute*) has attended to the story of Schmitt's emotional life the *Sonnets* presents, but I would like to comment on the way these poems move outward from that life to the shared traditions of poetic art.

The first poem is a good example of Schmitt's method. This sonnet attacks the scientific abstraction and detachment of the analyst's diagnoses in defense of the unknowable suffering of private experience. She makes the analytic process a struggle over words—the very first line concludes with "terminology." Words are the gatekeepers of psyche: hers the unsystematized inventions of a unique mind, his the coded terms of Freud's "talking cure." What the analyst might call Oedipal, Sonnet 1 rephrases: "Half myself lies under dirt and snow" with the body of her loved father. Yet at the same time, her defense of the private and the idiosyncratic incorporates wide swaths of cultural memory, beginning with Sophocles' presentation of Oedipus, and continuing with Ophelia's mad song from *Hamlet* ("They say the owl" continues "was a baker's daughter . . . we know what we are, but know not what we may be"), and King Lear's mad scene on the heath. She contends with the analyst, then, not only on behalf of her individual life, but on behalf of what she sees as the sedimented tradition of writing about and coming to terms with life. Her words, therefore, are not only her own, describing her individual insight and suffering, but her understanding of the words of a long, richly configured literary tradition. It is on this ground that she undertakes her debate with medical science.

The overarching structural device of the sequence, therefore, is that of a dialogue. On one level, the voices are those of the analyst (phrased, of course by the poet) and the analysand. These poems are preeminently intelligent about the process being undergone. She knows she must allow herself to be known, yet deeply fears being observed and understood—a "watchful and malign" face in the wallpaper of her childhood room/prison still haunts her (16). Only true intimacy could allow another to view her "proud soul naked"(19). The role given the analyst in this dialogue is caring, but his care is only "that [she] should sleep" (42). The edge repeated in many of the poems is that she wants his love in a way he cannot express it without relinquishing the power of his cure. She repeatedly calls him her "ghostly gigolo," using "ghostly" in a sense close to the locution "Holy Ghost," but calling up as well the earthly eroticism apparent in her latent transference love for him. Yet her skepticism about his "antiseptic" methods oscillates with her deep need for him to "hunt down" her mystery (3) and her gratitude for his care (4), which suggests that the persona in the sonnets is also in dialogue with herself.

On another level, the poet ventriloquizes the literature through which she had come to know herself before falling ill. This allusiveness is broad, rich, and passionate. In the end the persona in the poem is contending with herself, most particularly in the way 19, which accuses the analyst of taking money for his medical art, is answered by 20, in which she reminds herself that she too is paid for her pedagogical art. She feels shame that she pays to bare her soul to him, but she admits that she "pours her naked heart" into the teaching of Yeats's "Byzantium"; in both roles she bares her inmost self.

What I mean by calling her allusiveness broad can be demonstrated in a partial list. She alludes to Saint Augustine (10 his "brawny mind" as he recalled a childhood prank), the existentialist writers (13 "the no-God does not hear"), the New Testament (16 "I was in prison and ye visited me"), a black gospel song (17 "He never said another word no more"), the era of Joan of Arc (38 "the wolves are padding up the avenue"), the chambered nautilus (45 "the convoluted chambers of my brain"), and the barbarism of the Merovingian dynasty (57). Her largest and most overt debt, though, is to Shakespeare: *Lear* and *Hamlet* in 1, "patience on a monument" in 26, "How many noble selves did Shakespeare fling. . . ." in 47, play on the word "will" in 53, and two references to Lear's reply to Cordelia, "Nothing can come of nothing"—"that nothing pit whence all things spring" in 8 and "a nothing come to nothing in the mud" in 54. What is so impressive about this allusiveness is its complete fusion with the poet's self-probing. Her mind and heart seem to have been shaped by emotional as well as intellectual contact with other artists, especially with Shakespeare. The fact that Schmitt's persona here has read other writers with so much empathy and thought invites us to think and empathize with her.

The other notable debt to Shakespeare is her adaptation of his version of the sonnet form. To my ear, Schmitt's lines are so close to modern spoken English that the artfully filled out form disappears into condensed meaning, for example, "And cry for nothing as a baby cries (42), and "Said my 'Good night, then' in so many keys" (60). That's what artful form ought to do. I had to look closely to see the four-line quatrains and final couplets, with their nuanced repetitions and contrasts so much like Shakespeare's, in all 59 poems. Like him, she varies the tone and reference in the sequence; like his, her sequence tells a story in many keys; and like his, her themes circle around the large issues of sexual love and the passage of time.

Denis Donoghue describes the formal brilliance of literary art as "a sense of beauty that delights in the intrication of forms, the multiplicity of tones, and the daring with which an individual voice plays in clutter of allusions." These qualities characterize *Sonnets for an Analyst*.

—Peggy Knapp
Pittsburgh. Pennsylvania
October, 2003

# Sonnets for an Analyst

I do not buy your terminology.

A man is not a plaster skeleton,

And every phrase that turns him into one

Smells sure as Auschwitz of atrocity.

My father lies under the snow and dirt,

And half myself lies under dirt and snow.

Oedipal? But if Oedipus could know,

Poor blind old man, his eyesockets would smart.

Twenty-odd years I've lain in the bed I made:

"Love suffereth long, complaineth not, is kind."

Charity? No: a masochistic bind.

Chastity? No: turned off, withdrawn, afraid.

"They say the owl . . ." The girl's regressed, no doubt.

"Oh, howl, howl, howl . . ." Listen! Old Lear is acting out.

2

Come, ghostly gigolo. The night's half gone.

The Seconal has turned my blood to lead.

My hands are numb. I cannot tell my head

From the cold piece of palm it leans upon.

Come to these rooms, unpeopled, dispossessed

Of all I ever loved save only one,

And he a stranger now, and I alone,

Barbiturate rest presaging ultimate rest.

Come in your callow nattiness. Take in

My rumpled robe, my drugged and will-less sloth,

My meager flesh that scarcely lifts the cloth,

My skeleton that too much lifts the skin.

What do I want? Not servicing, not I.

Cry, take your glasses off for once and wipe them dry.

You should have laid the net more stealthily.

A beast twice taken is a wary beast,

Sees cord in velvety blackness, scents the pressed

Bruised plaintain and the broken timothy.

I watch in fear and see in your planned face

Remembered lights flick on and off again.

They'll focus, blinding white, and that spells pain,

Caged hunger, wordless begging, and disgrace.

Then could I still pull backward and wrench free?

What's on me here—a little harmless mud

Or clots of tepid, sticky, mortal blood

From old wounds torn by very memory?

Stay? Run? All reason's gone, the world's askew

When hunted says to hunter, "What am I to do?"

I have obscured your image with too much,

Your voice with sirens ripping through the night,

Your mouth with slackening lips fast going white,

Your hands with pitiful bones beyond all touch.

I have groped out for you where you were not:

What would you do in a torn envelope

That yielded the obituary of hope?

What, blighted, in a meal-dry flower-pot?

Now sanity intrudes. The mists tear loose.

Miasmal shifts stop dead, and what shows through,

Opaque, is an indubitable you

That leaves me much ashamed to make such use

Of what, if I had never fallen sick,

Would still have touched me—yes, and sweetly, to the quick.

They praise my house. Those friends who wish me well

Tell off my holdings: flowering shrubs and grass,

Marble, mahogany, linen, china, brass.

They cannot know, of course: my home's my hell.

They praise my work. What talent do I lack?

Not dignity, not casual eloquence,

Not patience with the arrogant or the dense.

They cannot know, of course: my work's my rack.

Then some poor girl who caught me in a sigh—

Herself bereft on earth—walks out with me,

Looks up, points up, makes sure that I will see

The wild, vast freedom of the winter sky.

But, child, the sky's blank, closed, impervious.

The sky is the shut lid of my sarcophagus.

This is a migraine (may you never know).

The candles on the table jerk and glare.

The guests are chirping waxworks with false hair;

Their artificial teeth chop row on row.

Then comes the nausea, then comes the pain.

Hideous to have eaten: what's inside—

Fish, flesh, or fowl—is something that has died

And yet to spew it up would split the brain.

The jiggling aura, silver, blue, and red,

Unstrings, benumbs, takes sight and thought away.

I drop my clattering fork. I think I say

"When do you sail?" or was it "Oh, my head"?

Rotting alive, I manage not to moan.

But, Christ, I envy rotting wood, dumb windworn stone.

I am a realist. Like that dour king
Whose motto "What Is, Is" was good enough
To get him through the common human stuff
Of causing—and enduring—suffering,
I have no use for dreams, and would not trade
Two bitter kisses in a dank garage,
Not for the most luxurious mirage
A practised masturbator ever had.
Who dreams such dreams outbids reality
And plans to pay his costs in counterfeit.
Since it was not, I'll not imagine it,
So beggaring truth. Let it suffice for me
That once when I stared blind through streaming grief
You handed me—you did—a paper handkerchief.

I think of him, I think of him asleep
Who made me out of wanting, slime, and air,
Whose uncouth beak and hollow cheeks I bear
Ungraciously. I think of him and weep.
Good gardener that he was, Time use his mould
As a rich marl for much engendering.
Deep in that nothing pit whence all things spring,
Give him a piece of wandering root to hold.
Dark upon dark, my blind heart stops on his.
My autumn knows his winter, scents my own,
Would hasten it, yearns greatly to step down
Where neither air nor slime nor wanting is.
And am I here, still shuddering on the steep
Raw edge? Shame, shame to wait and think of him and weep.

How like a child that cannot hear a rhyme
Re-said too often, how like some poor chit
Who makes the company dubious of her wit
By always harking back to one dear name,
I am tonight, save that I hold my tongue,
Well schooled in that pursuit by the hard years
I would have thought had dried such easy tears
As wash the unwrinkled eyelids of the young.
Pale on the carpet—pale but palpable—
Lies, in a ring of lamplight, your esteem.
It's there. No need to utter it. Serene
When the clock strikes, I will be capable
Of switching off the lamp. Ah, well . . . Ah, so
Age gives us all the grace to let a good thing go.

The world can never take a holiday

From metaphysical first principles.*

Even the raving, bolted in their cells

Have not the files to file these chains away.

Then how much less can I who rhyme and parse,

Expound and read and take a salary,

Call what goes posing as my probity

Anything other than a mawkish farce?

Bad wife in thought, bad friend in utterance,

Bad daughter, sister, mother—to the chin

I stand in sin and prate about my sin,

Chat of my weakness, point to circumstance,

And stroke and do not even bite the green

Hard pears that wrenched the brawny mind of Augustine.

* Alfred North Whitehead

My grandmother—I took her at her word—
Once told me, pointing at an awful page
Headed with thorns, that my unseemly rage
And puny lies could plague my dying Lord.

If she had turned our kitchen into hell
And set me naked at its hissing core
To drink no milk, no water, any more,
She'd scarce have served her purpose half as well.

Pity burst out of the torn womb with me.

Pity was in my playthings, in my bread.

Pity embraced His lacerated head;
And what more mean and loathsome could I be
Than a black fly hurtling through time and space
To buzz in an immortal and tormented face?

Strange, strange that I can reconstruct the scene:
The squares of sunlight in the modest aisles,
The offered hands, the cautious Lutheran smiles,
The woodwork varnished and the carpet clean.
And then a blackness like an open grave—
A black grilled square—the cellar showing through,
Nothing to start at, nothing queer or new,
Only a vent cut out to heat the nave.
I stop on a disintegrating chord
And say "Amen" and know that I will die,
That every verse and chapter hides a lie
To soothe a fool, that I have lost my Lord.
The rest is smashed, as if a great tree hurled
By wind crashed down on me, my Maker and the world.

Senseless, the stars collide, explode, and burn.

Careless, rank poison spreads in the atmosphere.

Mindless, the lion rends the blameless deer

And is devoured by sickness in his turn.

Heartless, the white come clawing at the black;

The yellow watch and bide their hour and sneer.

Useless we pray: the no-God does not hear.

Pointless we speak: the word comes bounding back.

Witless, the nations juggle fright and hate.

Planless, the clot that clogs an artery

Engenders slobbering insanity.

Heedless, the starving millions propagate

And sleep. Come, ghostly gigolo, and bless

This night with brainless aim-inhibited tenderness.

Yes, they were here, if separate from the rest,
Being so much together. Still, they ate
Our meat and bread and drank our wine and sat
Within our sight, her rough curls on his chest.
This form precludes a Prothalamion,
But I am glad that my unruly linnet
Has found a nest with a strong singer in it
And settles soft tonight, down against down.
What can I say? They knew what I would say
Were the world otherwise and I eloquent.
Old superstition watched until they bent
Their heads in lamplight, close to our bouquet,
And so were garlanded with the manifold
Oranges and yellows of my father's marigolds.

Deprived love is a sun that brings a drought:
All good green daily things are cracked and bled
And turned to metal in its molten red,

All saving springs scum over and dry out.
Deprived love makes a desert emptiness
Where bat-faced envy squeaks "With whom?" and "How?"
And swoops against the ear and chirps "Now! Now!"
Till the hot brain could burst for weariness.
Who uses deprivation as his cure
Puts cactus needles in a scorpion's bite
And has no further recourse but the night
That's sure to come to every sufferer.
Let me alone. I'm sick, I'm tired, I'm old.
I've died by fire three times. Please let me die of cold.

There was a window—high—I could not see.
The sun lay on the carpet—sourceless, wan—
A certain number of hours and then was gone.
I was in prison, and none visited me.
Up through the stairwell music came, and calls,
And the warm incense of the evening's spread.
I was alone. I ate my unblessed bread
Only with dolls and glass-eyed animals.
It was no dream. The wallpaper, intact,
Still shows the face that lurked in its design,
Coming and fading, watchful and malign.
I saw it, see it still. It is a fact;
Otherwise, would my eyes fill senselessly
To read: "I was in prison and ye visited me"?

Ill paid, ill used, ridiculously dressed
In the lean '30's, floating like a cork
Upon the churned, stained ebb-tide of New York,
I heard the murmurs of the much oppressed.
"Apples," they said, and "Pencils." Near fine shops
Where ermines coddled plaster mannikins
They stopped and asked for help; in rubbish bins
And garbage cans they poked for scraps and slops.
Once in the bowels of some dark building where
I waited for a man who held me light,
I heard one black, wild voice rip up the night
And counsel Christian patience in despair:
The night-turn janitor, swabbing up the floor,
Sang how *He never said another word no more.*

Like a strong undertow, unseen, that pulls

Seaweed in one direction, scatters shells,

Arranges sand and plankton, and compels

The startled fish to move in driven schools,

So does your will move through my darkest dark:

All talk, all thought, all casual actions flow

Fast, slow, east, west, as you would have them go.

Sleep works your purpose. Nightmares bear your mark.

Some wrecked intention with a salt-sheathed mast

Shuddered and fell apart, for you were there.

Lost coins turned over; ivory ribs heaved bare

Out of stirred sea-anemone. At last

A buoy-bell broke the dream and I awoke

And said . . . But then, who was it—I or you—who spoke?

I pay you, and it stabs me in my guts.

If I withheld the stipulated sum,

You would not listen, and I could not come.

You hear because I pay you, and it cuts.

I think of you, half waking, in the chill

Sobriety of dawn. I think of you

When twilight fades the sky to uncanny blue.

You think of me when I discharge my bill.

Oh, I could make a heap of currency

Under your nose and set a match to it.

Money—except to give away—is shit,

And money's all you want and have of me.

What shame it is to bribe a gigolo

To view a proud soul naked, you will never know.

Come, think some softer thought, my obdurate mind.

I draw my monthly wages, but to say

That all my doings are discharged with pay,

And thereby cancelled out, is to be blind.

My care for some plain student, dazed and lost,

My wonder when a thought breaks through a face,

Surcharging great young eyes with light and grace—

These are above and far beyond the cost.

It's not for dollars that I dare to pour

My naked heart into "Byzantium"—

There's shame and danger there to strike me dumb.

If you're a gigolo, then I'm a whore.

I never taught for money, never laid

My hand upon one head in order to be paid.

I was in Venice, in a delicate shower.

Small leaves, and wet, and waxen. Someone said,

"And will you go to see the holy dead

Under their ancient stones? Beside the tower

That guards their peace, see, too, the curious shrine

Built all of cedarwood." Through rain, I went

And drew into my nostrils a dry scent—

Parched petals powdered, incense, spices, wine—

Stronger as I drew close. I stepped inside

A church that held another and another,

And, in the aisle between each two, a Brother

Walked, with his rosary ringing at his side.

The third I could not enter: from its windows curled

Gold flame and that dry scent that sweetened all the world.

*A dream*

A doll within a doll within a doll:

Three neatly fitted wooden Russian peasants. . . .

She gave me that, one present and three presents;

She brought that home to me when I was small.

And cedarwood . . . what of the cedarwood?

Dry brown sachet, strewn on her underwear,

Touched to her elbows, brushed into her hair. . . .

Not cedarwood, but like it. . . . Sandalwood.

She moved within a cloud of fragrances.

No blossom-heavy, bee-inviting tree

Spread such a memorable scent as she,

Drawing me on to know her bounty. Yes,

Dog-tired, dog-cold, dog-thin, I yearn to rest

My head against the rounds of her warm powdered breast.


*An interpretation*

A thought within a thought within a thought . . .
And who can fathom it? The exhausted brain
Goes drowsing back to Venice in the rain,

Settles upon the sweet consuming spot
Where no one asks and no one tries to prove,
Where what is past is with us and the soul
Burns out to ash and rises phoenix-whole
From the unquenchable gold fire of love.
Christ, Jahveh, Buddha, and your master, though
At bitter enmity, make peace on this:
Where love is, there the living instant is
And death is not, nor mourning, but the flow
Of timeless giving. Look, I sought a tomb,
And generous sleep has given me a glowing womb.

And who put out my fire? I—even I,

That half of me that reasons and remembers.

Smell of stale smoke, sinister glare of embers,

And taste of ashes raised the hue and cry;

And what remained, I salvaged. What remains?

Our rubbish heap, burnt paper, a charred rafter.

Yes, and I naked, doubled up with laughter

That my own torch should burn away my brains.

Good God! I floundered in geometry,

Was weak in Latin, gullible with liars

And preachers, and unhandy with the pliers.

But how could I have lacked the acuity—

Burned thrice, burned to disfigurement and shame—

To see and recognize and stamp upon a flame?

I know the end of this limp comedy.

They've blabbed, a dozen other sufferers.

Boredom comes on, kind ennui that blurs

All but the flat, conclusive homily.

A year or so, and you'll bind up my pride,

Explaining how you could not love me: sure,

If you could love you could not work a cure:

Love's been withheld, love's never been denied.

I'll understand, or say I understand,

I'll parrot well about some wrong connection,

I'll not confuse refusal with rejection—

Or I will say I don't. I'll shake your hand

And leave, a vacant smile upon my lips

That proves me numb—oh, nicely—to the fingertips.

What in the interim shall I think of you
Who sit like patience on a monument,
Poured to the mould in Freudian cement,
Forever hearing out the fortunate few,
Dispensing mercy by the tick of clocks,
Eager to know and heal my bitter scar,
Yet prone to show it in your seminar—
What have I here? At best a paradox:
Soul-naked, yet well buttoned in a coat,
Warm like a friend, yet not at all a friend,
Strong to the end, yet eager for the end,
Close as the skin that's on me, yet remote.
I must confess I sometimes find them lewd—
Such cozy distance, such gregarious solitude.

Thinking now only of the end of it—

How will I die and wherefore have I been?—

I go, a transient, through the haunts of men

To my appointed seat. A hypocrite

Behind a desk, with shaking hands and knees,

I pass what's ceased to serve me to the young,

Telling them coldly, with a stony tongue,

What Jesus said, and Kant and Socrates.

Now that love's gone, with sun and eyes put out,

I plumb such primal dark as was before

My mindless forebears heaved themselves ashore

And dully pulsed and numbly turned about

Eyeless toward nothing, but without the wit

To know what waited for them at the end of it.

What serpent's poison struck through what you said?

I entered human, and I turned aside

Dreadful, a walking corpse wound up to stride

Over the faces of the quick and the dead.

My ears are deafened by an inward roar.

My speech is mangled by my grinding jaws.

My fists are hammers and my fingers claws.

Whatever is, I will to be no more.

I hate, I hate, and nothing is exempt,

No, not the holiest winged remembrances;

I strangle and befoul them where they press

Against my brain; I rend them in contempt.

Let me have limitless vengeance, let me treat

My heart, your heart, all hearts like so much butcher's meat.

The innocent pigeons flown from lands long lost

With dead men's letters fastened to their feet—

I broke their necks and flung them to the heat,

I gave their bodies to the holocaust.

And they are dead and blackened, meat and skin.

They will not come again. I need not wait,

Drowsing, to hear them pecking at the gate

Or rise and go in sleep to let them in.

Their missives with their feathers fed the blaze.

Yet here and there between the drifts of smoke

I saw a phrase: She sang . . . He wept . . . We spoke . . .

It bloomed . . . Forgive . . . They knew . . . a psalm of praise . . .

The rest is charred. I look at you aghast:

How, in these ashes, could you find my past?

I could refuse to answer. Like the snow,
Silence could mound me round and dignify
The shale-sharp anger and the ragweed lie,
The bones, the seeds, what rots, what still might grow—
But not at zero or at ten below.
Taking my coloring from the vacant sky,
I could lie blank until the day I die,
And you could always ask and never know.
I could be mute and strike one sparrow blind,
Keep him too dazed to fly away or light,
Hold him still fluttering over vapid white,
Baffle and craze him with that woman's mind,
That woman's soul, that spurious mystery
Which all men want and no man ever had of me.

Say I was wronged; say Faith and two wronged men
Connived to wrong me. Is that balm to spread
Upon a corpse? Can virtue raise the dead?
Say I was wronged, and fifty times again
Repeat the incantation—it's all one,
I still lie stark and sightless to the dawn,
My heart a stone and all my good years gone:
However it was done, I am undone.
Your insistent voice comes faintly through a shroud,
"Who bears the blame—forsaker or forsaken?"
What difference does it make? Can I awaken,
Flex my stiff arms and legs, hold high and proud
My bludgeoned head because the slaying's stain
Lies more upon the slayer than upon the slain?

It was no war. It was an accident.

When two good ships converge in the fog and strike

Athwart each other, which is wrong, which right?

Where is there substance for an argument?

Madwoman that I am, from sun to sun

I call on God to judge, I fulminate;

But God's not God if He'll negotiate

Between two blind souls in collision.

After the shuddering impact and the cry,

Here on the cluttered water, with the gulls

Swooping amazed over the shattered hulls

And tangled rigging, what could signify

Less than whose flag flaps last above the brine

In brief and senseless victory—his flag or mine?

She owes me rent, that fierce preposterous woman

Who bore and mauled the one I thought was mine.

She's here with me out of her grave: malign,

Ubiquitous, invulnerable, inhuman.

I bathe my body, and she mocks my breasts;

I stir against him, and she tweaks the sheet;

I eat and taste her poison in the meat;

I serve and see her sneering at the guests.

No voice of mine could drown her long harangue.

She moulds me in her image—small-eyed, old

And shrewd. If I could break her stranglehold,

I'd only stumble on her noose and hang.

Get at me then, and soon, foul visitor.

I'm much too tired to elude you any more.

That he should lay her mask on me is human:
We all grope backward toward the sheltering womb,
Touch the dead flower in the living bloom—
I cannot have a man not born of woman.

That he should add her voice to mine is well;
Without some resonance any voice is weak,
But hers—let God bear witness—was a shriek,
An imprecation, an appeal to hell.

And that I take chastisement for her flaws,
Blame for her lovelessness, I find too hard.
She raged, I fed stray cats in the back yard;
She struck for blood and I filed down my claws.

No, it is cruelty, it is harsh excess
To beat a cringing dog as if she were a lioness.

The fifteenth Louis, cold and prurient,

Yet found his hearthfire in the Pompadour

And combed the brothels for his ease no more

But talked in praise of "something permanent."

And when, disabled by an early blight,

She could no longer clasp him thigh on thigh,

He kept her still in honor at Versailles,

He stopped with her to talk and say good night.

His mind, an icy crystal, lost its edge

Over her yellowed neck and faded curls.

He cherished her—for all his "little girls."

Seeing her hearse move past the formal hedge,

He wept—our only record of his tears—

And said, "There goes a friend, a friend for twenty years."

Cool through the grass of Eden, two abreast,
They trailed their blameless, undirected feet,
Took what they thought was sweet and proved it sweet,
Passed guiltless from fulfillment into rest.
No hard parental counsel intervened,
Shrinking the breast and chilling the cupped hand.
No birth-cord dragged them each from each to stand
Divided, shaken, stricken, and obscene.
No one was by demanding that their eyes
Turn from each other long enough to see
The death-pangs of an old, doomed loyalty:
Their undented bellies were their Paradise.
No, only Eve and Adam loved each other—
She fashioned from his bone, and he without a mother.

Go at me then, my soul's geologist.

Dig to the bottom of this layered lie

That other men call "she" and I call "I,"

Passive as earth, a weak antagonist.

Dig through the soil where gentle green things grow,

Where scholars stroll and eager children run,

Dig to the clay of fear shut out from the sun,

Bone-packed, the primal sepulchre, below.

Dig on through the obsidian of my anger,

Fit stuff for arrows shaped to maim and kill.

What, are you sweating? Come, dig further still

Through the black diorite that is my hunger.

And then I give; you come upon the core

And it is need, red need that can be slaked no more.

When Joan was still a child in Domremy,
France was so bled by famines and defeats
That wolves walked nightly in the Paris streets
And glared gold-eyed at men and would not flee.
The wilderness possessed the citadel;
And this is Doomsday manifested when
Nothing is outlawed, none a citizen
Of anything except a common hell.
Before my war, I had an urban brain,
Civil and bounded, orderly and mild.
My gates shut out what slavered and ran wild,
My watchfires burned against the black terrain.
The locks are off, the faltering embers few,
And wolves are padding up the avenue.

I thought I waited in a place of going,

A shed of glass pressed in upon my mist.

Many were there. The kissing and the kissed

Stood to their knees in crumpled paper blowing;

Many and more than many, dressed in shrouds,

Took up old coats and bags made fast with strings.

The roar of engines and the wind of wings

Bore down upon us from the milky clouds.

And one—oh, grave, known face—turned in the queue

That walked into the void, and neither smiled

Nor raised his workworn hand to greet his child,

But went his way unseeing; and I knew,

Since you had cured me of the leprous sore

By which he knew me once, he knew me now no more.

I mourn her, too, the old All Fools' Day queen

Whose soul was stitched of brilliant rags and patches,

Whose mind was insight flung in bits and snatches—

Bitter confetti, pink and arsenic green.

I mourn her clutter, her scatology,

The noisy hymns she used to sing in Lent,

The garbled Gospel texts, the irreverent

Elbow with which she nudged the Deity.

I mourn her jelly glasses—cherry, quince;

I mourn her peppermints, her licorice drops.

I mourn her clay-bound touch. My mourning stops

On ulcerous self-recrimination, since

I gave her, paralysed, to charity,

And when I was a child she fought and wept for me.

How—how, if love and hate so intertwine—
Can I tell kindness from a guilty ache,
Sort out the poisoning berry from the grape,
Hack out, drag out the rankness from the vine?
If thirty years have fused two vines in one,
To separate them is to rip and mangle
In hopes of salvaging a limp green tangle
That's doomed to wilt at the first touch of the sun.
I wake in smothering blackness with my head
Too far from his. I do not hear his breath.
I wait, hear, smile: he's mine, still mine, not death's.
But why the fear? Oh, could I wish him dead?
Shame—and more shame to take his warmth when he
Will wake an hour from now in the same fright for me.

What you have given me, I have carried off

And made good use of in another bed.

Yet there's remorse: I cannot put my head

Right on the pillow, cannot huddle soft

Against the long-known body. Tight and small

I make my fists and thrust them in my eyes

And cry for nothing as a baby cries.

If all is right that is connubial,

Why am I shamed and how am I untrue?

You do not want and cannot use my need,

The seed you give me is a different seed,

Still, still my spasm's traitorous to you.

Still, still I cannot fathom out your deep

Uncaring care that only wants that I should sleep.

You laugh, and a twin prodigy takes place.

First, that long laughter—schooled? spontaneous?

But seldom sprung between the two of us—

Breaks up the pious contours of your face.

Then, in myself there is a ringing noise:

Smoked glass is smashed, a grimy pane and whorled

Cracks, and I sight an undistorted world,

Clean blue and silver, through the airy voids.

I said my *mea culpa* and you laughed.

Are you a man to laugh at the accursed

Choking on sulphur? Scarcely. At the worst

You take me to be amiably daft.

Schooled or spontaneous, I like you well

Convivial priest, light-hearted harrower of hell.

If every wish were father to an act,
What man could leave his house in the dark and come
Full circle round a city block back home

Penis and purse and mortal skin intact?
And I myself, public and vilified
A little more than most, would stand in mud
Up to my waist, empurpled in my blood,
My hide as riddled as Sebastian's hide.
Yet we have May and peace. Men look and lust
And keep their hungry palms from neighbors' wives.
Few are the bullets, very few the knives
That taste of human flesh before they rust.
And what I wished—frail, discontinuous,
Father to nothing—looks at worst ridiculous.

The convoluted chambers of my brain
House a high retinue uniquely mine.
No other mind can copy or design
The subtle, various doings of my train.
New in the universe and singular
Are these my christening feasts and burials;
Matchless contentions, peerless carnivals
Move echoing round my skull and stir my hair.
Yet any brow laid open would expose
A complex and astounding spectacle.
The meanest head houses a miracle
That goes irrevocably when it goes.
The single fact that dignifies my place
Is that you took a room, you lived in it a space.

In Lisbon, when the erratic tidal flow
Undid what was not toppled by the quake,
They shook off shock and made what they could make:
Stark streets, blank squares, poor houses dull and low.
And every boatman poling through the mire
Knew sickening disappointment and disgrace
To see the drab, flat line of roofs replace
The Moorish portico and Gothic spire.
I have survived a microcosmic shock:
My bells are cracked, my avenues awry,
My cannon drenched and pointed at the sky.
Soaked rubble trips me everywhere I walk.
I cannot mourn the rift in a hallowed wall
Or mend quaint saints. The marvel is I build at all.

How many noble selves did Shakespeare fling
To death against the gimcrack scenery
So that his emptied husk might hold to see
The green of Stratford through another spring.
How many Christs were flogged and nailed and hung—
In oil on wood or canvas—so that Bosch
Could draw his draught of yellow beer and slosh
The fiery ghost of life around his tongue.
Oh, we are fools to send such deputies
Ahead of us to death. Could we devise
A shabbier joke than to materialize
In our hunched greyness after such as these?
Brave Tristan died—he could have done no less—
And shoddy Wagner lived to dwindle on success.

This is no place for pruning. Passages
Shut off by tangled hopes and twisted needs
Yield you your patterns. He who clips and weeds
Cuts out your signs, uproots your purposes;
And I who cannot let green chaos spread
Work nightshift to thin out and shape the thick
Rank overgrowth, and waken on a click:
Incriminating scissors in my head.
But I have walked in these same woods in the sweet
Season of May, have thought these boughs were soft,
Have run upon them and been caught aloft
Out of my element and off my feet—
Not borne upon a cloud, but dangling numb
From the chin, a stiffening body, like poor Absalom.

The thunder rattles like loose sheets of tin.

The lightning flicks like crazy neon lights.

Drawing the drapes against brash blacks and whites,

I settle for the sober golds within.

He sits and reads. I work with cloth and thread

And scarcely smell soaked grass. We count the cost

In terms of stems snapped off and blossoms lost

In a sedate, expensive flowerbed.

Yet I remember herds of god-bred colts

Whinnying down the wind, wild wants laid bare

Lordly and reckless in the violet glare

Of Zeus the father's splendid thunderbolts,

And we two, all oblivious of these,

Standing, drenched mouth to mouth, among torn peonies.

I am God's dray-horse, whom He has forgot.

Winded, in blinders—yes, and terrified

As if His whip were biting through my hide—

I haul His rubbish to a vacant lot.

Heavy the scrap-iron of His former wrath.

Filthy the rags of His old mercies. Cold

The crust of His last supper gone to mould—

The smell of it, the taste of it is death.

God's trash bears witness that the time has come

For the fresh dispensation, the new Word.

If He has spoken it, I have not heard.

I am his dray-horse. Deaf and blind and dumb,

I must go down as His old Law goes down.

*Kyrie, eleison. Christe, eleison.*

What once was is irrevocably gone.

The ache that was forever, the iron ache

Dissolves now as completely as the flakes

That melt away on their memorial stones.

My hand, a liar, drained of tenderness,

Fondles their relics falsely, falsely falls

On clothes—untenanted materials,

On mirrors—placid, vacant, imageless.

The time is come when even I must cease,

Must leave off fasting and sit down and eat

Meat without gall, yes, and enjoy the meat,

Warm in a kind of wan and witless peace,

As though my dead had counted till I shed

My thousandth tear, and, satisfied, were dead.

Lord, Lord, I grieve because I cannot grieve.

How can I live the length of Holy Week

And not climb past the serried stones to seek

What carping reason says I ought to leave?

Not step upon the porous turf again?

Not throw away the withered Christmas wreath?

Not kneel above the sunken crooks to breathe

Cold essence of a graveyard cyclamen?

Since I have journeyed down an endless road

With a scant armful, I have little left

To lose. Bereaved that I am not bereft—

Since even pain is something—I am loath

To drop an ear from my diminished sheaf,

Even a blasted ear whose only yield is grief.

52

The voice goes first: I cannot hear you speak.

It's so with the long-absent and the ones

Gone down beyond the reach of snows and suns;

Greek poets said they chirped and called them weak.

The voice goes first—fades, falters, is not heard.

My mother, newly buried, in my sight

Ironed, cooked, pulled back the catch, turned on the light,

And fed the cat, but never said a word.

If you are what I wish, as you have said,

God knows my wishing is beyond my knowing.

Needing you, could I wish to see you going?

Living within you, could I wish you dead?

If this is of my willing, kill my will;

My will's my enemy; it wills me only ill.

He did not love me. Had the April bud
Been penetrated by that blasting fact,
It would have dropped, its sticky coating cracked,
A nothing come to nothing in the mud.
He could not love me. Had the August flower—-
Fragile and succulent and richly sapped—
Been struck with that report, it would have snapped
And curled and decomposed within the hour.
He would not love me. If the autumnal burr
Had taken that impact, its unready seeds
Would have been rattled out among the weeds—
Green wastage that no spring could disinter.
He never loved me; and the day arrived
When I was old and dry, and knew it, and survived.

Bach, seated ponderous in the sunset nave,
Cudgelled his heart to conjure from the keys
His old expected Sabbath prodigies:
The Margrave specified, the hireling gave.
Week after week he fed them to the choir—
The peerless counterpoint, the crowding notes,
A wine that should have scorched their stolid throats,
A seraph's draught of honey mixed with fire.
Who heard? Who cared? The yawners in the aisles
Drowsed through an hour of the usual stuff
Gone out of fashion, though well-wrought enough.
Perhaps the magpies, blasted from their tiles
By some great shuddering arpeggio,
Sailed through the blueness, shrieking, "Father, do You know?"

Breath, thought, dreams, gestures—everything I am—
Is fed through the cold tick of the machine
And issues from it meaningless and mean:

A jerking scrawl across a cardiogram.
Love, poison love that has no antidote,
Dissolves with flesh under the crimson ray
And registers nothing in the usual grey
Skeletal shadow on the fluoroscope.
Even my charged heart gets a Latin name,
Becomes a big flawed muscle, wanting tone,
Stammering and laboring in its cage of bone.
How long? For what? Who cares? It's all the same.
And yet so long as I have eyes to see,
So long this lives, and this gives back myself to me.

I hear the ancient Merovingian brawl

Ranting and staggering through the elegance:

Barbarians gone rotten, arrogance

Galled by old feuds and hot with alcohol.

Their eyes protrude. Their foreheads shine with grease.

They quote the price of emeralds and fur,

Trip up the doings of the caterer,

And shriek approval of the centerpiece.

One takes his uncle's character apart;

One corners a young wife and gets his feel;

A third describes his cleverest, vilest deal;

And nothing dies but innocence and the heart.

No poison brewed, no mace on hand to give

The coup de grâce, and all those sordid years to live.

Here are his pictures, both in newsprint. I

Have never merited a photograph.

Here—yellowed—he puts down a knowing laugh.

There—current—he expels a puzzled sigh.

Oh, and the line has slipped, the mouth has slipped.

Age, worry, grief have worked that mouth of his

Out of all prospect of a driving kiss:

Most mild, most curiously tender-lipped.

So much at least we share, being separate—

We and the tortoises and the parade

Of gods on a Peruvian façade—

We all go soft, we all disintegrate;

So cools the white star subtly in the west,

So subtly slips the line of this my drying breast.

There was a fox who lost his tail; astute

Enough to profit by predicament,

He called his betters to a parliament,

Displayed his loss, and urged they follow suit.

I—long on mutilation, short on gall—

Withdrew; but I was singularly deft

At finding other scrawny beasts, bereft,

Trapped, shot, starved, mangled, sorry creatures all.

Feeble and pusillanimous, we fled

Battle, and lived on carrion in holes;

And weird transvaluations in our souls

Made us talk strangely, shamefully. We said:

"How holy is the cold, uncaring mind!

How beautiful are the trembling eyelids of the blind!"

I have devised so many ways to die—
Green vertigo spun out to emptiness,
Enclosed combustion and the boiling hiss,
Lethargic torpor like the autumn fly's;
Foreseen such shameful ends to my affairs—
This work cut off, that quarrel unreconciled,
These rooms in squalor, those reports unfiled
To plague unloving aggravated heirs;
Said my "Good night, then" in so many keys—
Confused, in paroxysms of derision
Ingathering into one penumbral vision
All doors, streets, towns, all clouds and spires and seas
That I can mock my mawkishness: Oh, come,
Sure, sure, we all owe God a death, but only one.

Preposterous . . . a clot of sentient cells
Buoyed on womb-water, wrapped around in night,
Hurled out against the thrust of cold and light,
Salt taste of blood, shrill voices, stifling smells;
Aware of self—eyes, feet, nose, belly—tense
Grip on the finger, gums clamped round the breast,
Dream images behind the lids, no rest,
Prisoned in flesh, prisoned in sentience;
Self-sated, straining out to span the chasm,
To escape the sensate self no matter how—
The usual way will do it: brow to brow
And thigh to thigh in one black brainless spasm,
Spawning more cells; so tricked, superfluous,
Alone, disintegrating . . . oh, preposterous.

Make me a larva. Spin a thick cocoon
Between me and my outraged sense of wrong,
Bed me in filaments. Sing me a song,
Tuneless, since there is reason in a tune.
Seal up the apertures of sense, and when
The generative night exudes perfume
Preserve me innocent in my downy gloom
Of what's a cruel goad to beasts and men.
Send me a saving freeze out of the north
To end me in my sleep, to make me less
Than even a larva. Make me nothingness,
Immune to growth, immune to going forth,
Excused from resurrection. Put me by.
I will not issue, no, not even as a butterfly.

Your body's yours, your calling notwithstanding.

Not the technique nor the remitted fee

Nor my stern need gives me the liberty

To force upon you my inexpert handling.

To fantasy that you will dance my dance

Is gross and tyrannous. I exorcize

Such dreams before they clot behind my eyes

Or thicken in a hypnogogic trance.

Unasked-for ardor's outrage; and a thought

Perceived and blabbed, according to our pact,

Fleshes itself between us, is an act,

Grabs what it wants, and what you owe me not.

Your body's yours, yours to bestow or keep.

Keep it. I do not steal, not even in my sleep.

Son of Hippocrates, you make me sick,
The lamp you carry through my winding dark
Is trimmed too neatly to let off a spark.
It burns, but with a disinfected wick.
You're not involved. Sworn to a higher hope,
You set contagious mortal care outside:
Ardor might smash the creature on the slide,
A passionate breath would blur the microscope.
You do not pity. What is pitiful
Would be beneath such singular skill as yours;
And I'm superior matter, which insures
That even my vomit is respectable.
What's washed so clean—as Henry James once said—
Under the sterile laboratory tap, is dead.

Since I have swallowed such anomalies—
Worms, bits of tinfoil, half a yard of cord,
The executed body of my Lord,
The lavish dinners of my enemies,
White slippery lies and sticky blandishments,
My tainted love flung back for me to eat,
My rival's patent joy in my defeat,
The knowing critic's cool indifference;
Since I have downed the closing of a hearse,
The springs of passion turned to sewers of shame,
The sick monotony—all days the same,
The mindless chaos of the universe,
How is it that I cannot take this small
Pink heap of twenty tasteless Seconal?

The Frisian king at the baptismal font
Only half heard the monkish homily.
His fen-bred sight roved up and down to see
What splendors would be stored to his account:
The Mays of heaven laid on in white and red,
An ivory throne draped in unblemished wool,
Cool lilies dripping in a silvered pool—
And suddenly he bethought him of his dead.
And tentatively, hoping for the best,
He said, "My forebears—tell me where they sit,"
And got his answer: "In the flaming pit
Of hell," and left, unsprinkled and unblessed.
Nor is it written that the monks that night
Wept for the sinning sires that sowed them into light.

And I have seen her tangled in that net—
Caught and exultant, hurt and glorying—
Have cried for her and said "Poor thing, poor thing,"
Have gone to sleep, pillow and knuckles wet;
Have started up in webby light to see
Rags of a dream that conscience tore to bits—
Your grizzled chest under my fingertips;
Have cried again—for whom?—for me, for me.
Never and nothing. Not the transitory
Blaze in the locked-up office or motel.
No note, no call. No portion in her hell,
Her blossoming hell. No portion in her glory.
So far I love—no more. Pull in your breath
And let it out and talk my love to death.

Entirely too much is made of it—
Volumes of civil law and canon law,
Stunned Reverends that freeze or hem and haw,
Boys who explode in pornographic wit,
Counselors trained in hypocritical talk,
Spinsters who peer and say "Pull down your dress,"
Wives outraged, shamefaced husbands in distress,
Parents who pace the floor till two o'clock,
The gossip's eye a moist and glinting slit,
The writhed lips whispering behind the hand
"Ask *me*. I know. I saw . . . you understand"—
Entirely too much is made of it
That any two agree in any weather
To fit their gross and rebel parts together.

If God is dead, then show me to his grave.

Not that I hope to hear beneath that rock

A strangled voice make necromantic talk

Or feel the stir of the Ephesian wave

Or conjure a revived automaton.

Skeleton of man's murdered hope, receive

The only grace I have, the grace to grieve

Without the drugs of self-deception.

At the bald center of our wilderness,

Before earth shrivels up and oceans freeze,

Let me get down lamenting on my knees,

A nothing keeping watch with nothingness.

Considering the millions who were born

To sing *Te Deum* here, one soul should stay to mourn.